Perth and the South-West

a panoramic gift book

Steve Parish

Contents

Perth

from the heart

When I arrive in Perth, or its companion port, Fremantle, I am always struck by the intense quality of the light. Trees, gardens, river, buildings and sea reveal themselves in brilliant colours and subtle hues, every detail seen clearly through air free from smoke or haze. These cities on the Swan River are wonderful places in which to live or holiday, full of friendly people and fascinating sights. They are particularly beautiful in spring and summer, when public parks and private gardens are ablaze with wildflowers. The whole South-West of Western Australia echoes the themes of beauty and hospitality. I hope this book helps you discover the magic of Perth and the South-West.

Steve Parish

Riverside City

life on the Swan

Perth extends over the coastal plain of the Swan River. Its eastern suburbs nestle against the Darling Range escarpment; its western suburbs border the Indian Ocean. The port of Fremantle stands at the mouth of the Swan, some 15 kilometres down river from the heart of Perth. Northwards, the city stretches over the sandy coastal plain to Yanchep.

Captain James Stirling and free settlers founded Fremantle and Perth in 1829. The new colony survived many hardships, alleviated first by the arrival of convicts and later by the discovery of gold. Later mineral discoveries added to the State's prosperity.

Today, Perth and Fremantle are flourishing and self-sufficient cities supporting around 1.5 million people. Great cultural diversity adds to the richness of lifestyle. The marvellous climate – hot, dry summers and crisp winters – is perfect for popular outdoor activities like sailing, sport, alfresco dining and coastal touring.

Perth city seen from the air.

The spectacular tower of the Swan Bells stands in Barrack Square. It allows the public to see bells and change ringers in action.

Perth

– the sights

The glittering tower of the Swan Bells houses the 250-year-old bells of St Martin-in-the-Fields. A gift to the city of Perth to mark Australia's bicentenary, they are now a landmark at Old Perth Port.

The Swan Bells and Barrack Street, viewed over the jetties of Old Perth Port.

The graceful spire encloses a working peal of 18 bells.

Stained-glass magnificence, Forrest Chase Shopping Centre.

Forrest House, a reconstruction of Alexander Forrest's residence, in Perth city.

Wesley Uniting Church, with towering Central Park in the background.

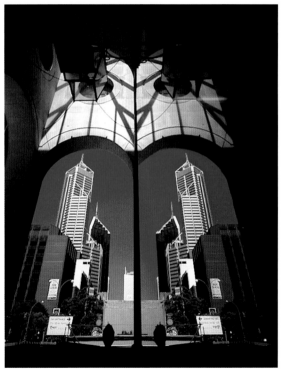

Mirror-images of Central Park, Perth's tallest building.

Shopping in London Court, a mock-Tudor lane built in 1937.

London Court's entrance – Claude De Bernales created this delightful fantasy.

Old Perth Boys' School, built between 1852 and 1854.

Perth Town Hall rises at the eastern end of Hay Street Mall.

Silver Gulls fly past Burswood International Resort and Casino, on the Swan River.

Black Swans, bird emblem of Western Australia, on the Swan River.

Citizen of the Year Lake, Burswood Park.

Pleasure craft moored on the Swan River at Matilda Bay, Crawley.

Having fun on the Swan River.

Perth Mint is Australia's oldest operating mint.

Residential development in East Perth.

Grand Winthrop Hall at the University of Western Australia.

The Narrows Bridge links South Perth to Mounts Bay Road and the city.

A view across the city to Perth Water and South Perth.

Kings Park

a floral fantasy

Since 1872, four hundred hectares of bushland on the heights of Mt Eliza, overlooking the river and Perth city, have gradually been developed as one of the world's most remarkable parks. Kings Park has areas of native bushland, green lawns, avenues of stately trees, war memorials, the fine Fraser's Restaurant and a complex of picnic and playground areas. It also offers magnificent views of the city and river. However, the crowning glory of this reserve is the display of native wildflowers to be enjoyed in the bush and in the Botanic Gardens.

Western Australia is the home of many endemic flowering plants and the gardens are fascinating at any time of year. Springtime displays and the Wildflower Festival that is held each September bring unequalled splendour to the park.

Perth city seen from Kings Park.

Kings Park, overlooking Perth, is the site of the State War Memorial and the Flame of Remembrance.

Top and above: An Australian garden, complete with Hills Hoist, at the Wildflower Festival.

Kangaroo Paws and Everlasting Daisies create a stunning display at the Kings Park Wildflower Festival.

Floral fantasy in the Wildflower State.

Fringed Mantis Orchid
Caladenia dilatata var. *falcata*

Rose Mallee
Eucalyptus rhodantha

Pink Everlasting Daisy
Rhodanthe chlorocephala var. *rosea*

Hood-leaved Hakea
Hakea cucullata

Geraldton Wax
Chamelaucium uncinatum

Red and Green Kangaroo Paw
Anigozanthos manglesii

Queen of Sheba Orchid
Thelymitra variegata

Pink Rice Flower
Pimelea ferruginea

Crimson Kunzea
Kunzea baxteri

Many-flowered Fringe Lily
Thysanotus multiflorus

Lilac Hibiscus
Alyogyne huegelii

Cranbrook Bell
Darwinia meeboldii

Mountain Grevillea
Grevillea alpina

Cowslip Orchid
Caladenia flava

Albany Blackbutt
Eucalyptus staeri

Cow Kicks
Stylidium schoenoides

Fireworks illuminate the Swan River.

The lights of Perth city, seen from Fraser Avenue, Kings Park.

Southern Hairy-nosed Wombat

Gidgee Skink, western form.

One of the zoo's tigers on the prowl.

Perth Zoo

wild wonderland

Perth Zoo is in South Perth, reached by bus or by ferry from the Barrack Street Jetty. The zoo's mission "To advance the conservation of wildlife and to change community attitudes towards the preservation of life on Earth" is reflected in the exhibits housing native and exotic creatures in conditions that replicate their natural habitats.

The Numbat is one of Australia's rare marsupials. It eats only termites.

The entrance to Perth Zoo.

A Growing City

movement north and south

Perth's most rapid expansion is to the north and south along a sand plain bordered by the Darling Scarp and the Indian Ocean. New developments make the most of the sea and the remaining freshwater lakes along the coastal strip.

Sculpture and grass-trees adorn a traffic island in Joondalup.

Joondalup locals gather around the jetty to observe each other and feed... or be fed.

Mindarie Keys Harbour Estate and Marina.

Lakeside Joondalup Shopping City.

Perth Beaches

the great aquatic lifestyle

Perth's beaches are marvellous, both in quality and in location. They are stretches of pure silver sand sloping gently to an ocean that is the delight of swimmers, surfers and sailors. And they form a chain in which the central links are just a short drive from the city centre.

A groyne shelters swimmers at Cottesloe.

Silver sand and cool ocean at City Beach.

Cottesloe is one of Perth's favourite family beaches, with excellent facilities, grassy areas for picnics and top restaurants and cafés.

An aerial view south over Scarborough Beach towards Floreat and City Beaches. All are within easy reach of the city centre.

Summer is bliss on Perth's beaches, but they are used for recreation year-round.

Observation City Complex at Scarborough Beach.

The beaches north and south of Hillarys Boat Harbour are ideal for sea sports.

Hillarys Marina is part of the Hillarys Boat Harbour–Sorrento Quay complex.

Visiting Perth AQWA at Hillarys Boat Harbour is a great experience.

The Quokka, a small wallaby, lives in large numbers on Rottnest.

Wadjemup Lighthouse with the Rottnest Lakes in the background.

A view across Bathurst Point and Bathurst Lighthouse
to Thomson Bay Settlement, Rottnest Island.

Rottnest Island

a unique environment

The seventeenth-century Dutch navigator Willem de
Vlamingh named the island just off the mouth of the
Swan River "Rottnest", or rats' nest. The creatures
he thought were rats were actually small wallabies,
the Quokkas, which still flourish on Rottnest Island, a
popular holiday and day-tripping destination.

No private cars are allowed on Rottnest, so everyone
walks or cycles. Many buildings have historic interest
and the beaches and bays around the coast are
paradise for swimmers and divers: some of the world's
southernmost coral reefs are found here.

The island's history is rich, particularly the Aboriginal
connections. One of the most fascinating heritage trails
traces the many shipwrecks around the coast.

Fremantle

a historic hub

As the site of the America's Cup Challenge in 1987, the port city of Fremantle gained an international reputation as a tourist destination. Today, it is a cosmopolitan city with maritime charm, home to a multicultural and artistic community. Its bistros and restaurants are deservedly famous.

Many Fremantle buildings have been beautifully renovated.

Top and above: Contrasts in building decoration, Fremantle.

Elegant buildings in the local limestone stand in the port area.

Preceding pages: Looking across Success and Fishing Boat Harbours to Fremantle Harbour.
Above: Fremantle's South Terrace "cappuccino strip".

Fremantle Town Hall and a Fremantle Scenic Tram.

Top and above: Enjoying Fremantle, a relaxed and friendly city.

To the North

the road to Nambung

The 250-kilometre drive north of Perth to Nambung National Park is particularly delightful in spring and early summer, when wildflowers blossom in roadside bushland. At any time of the year the limestone pillars called the Pinnacles inspire fascination. They have been used as background to fashion photographs and feature films.

A dilapidated cottage adds a rustic touch.

Wildflower splendour covers the coastal plains north of Perth.

Yellow Everlasting Daisies blanket the plains.

Nambung National Park is famous for the Pinnacles, pillars of limestone exposed by shifting sand dunes.

The country north of Perth is wildflower-embroidered sandplains and tranquil farmland. The Great Northern Highway leads through the wine country of the Swan Valley to New Norcia, a monastery established in 1846 by Spanish Benedictine monks. The museum and art gallery feature works by Spanish and Italian masters.

Above: Colourful murals decorate houses and buildings in the area.

The Benedictine Monastery at New Norcia has 27 National-Trust-classified buildings.

Green pasture in the Avon Valley, north-east of Perth.

The Busselton Jetty is said to be the longest timber jetty in Australia.

A Bunbury mural pays homage to marine life.

The South-West

a relaxing paradise

Bunbury, a major port south of Perth, is Western Australia's second largest town. It has everything the holiday-maker could desire, including dolphins that visit Koombana Beach. Busselton, a popular resort just 50 kilometres further south, is named after the Bussells, a pioneer family in the district. Either town makes a good base for exploration of the south-west coast.

Sculptures at a Bunbury intersection watch over the Rose Hotel.

A souvenir of happy days at Bunbury.

Scenes from Margaret River, famous for its wineries. The vintages produced in this South-West town are eagerly sought after worldwide.

Anglers try their luck, Margaret River.

A gracious homestead at Gilgarad.

Margaret River

Margaret River is one of the South-West's most delightful centres, known for fine wines, gourmet delights, and marvellous surf. The area is home to many artists and craftspeople. Within Margaret River's surrounds are fossil caves, magnificent forests and abundant wildlife and wildflowers.

Leeuwin-Naturaliste National Park

Named after the ships of early Dutch and French navigators, Leeuwin-Naturaliste National Park protects a 120-kilometre strip of scenic grandeur, shaped by westerly winds and ocean swells, from Bunker Bay to Augusta. Rugged cliffs and sheltered, sandy beaches make up the shoreline. Inland, cave systems carved by water from the coastal limestone underlie forests that include tall Karri trees, as well as unique Jarrah and Marri.

Mammoth Caves have been the site of fossil finds.

Cape Leeuwin Lighthouse stands on the southernmost promontory of Leeuwin–Naturaliste National Park.

Young Karri trees stand amidst green fern fronds.

A historic steam engine at the timber town of Pemberton.

Pelicans gather around a fisherman preparing his nets, Wilsons Inlet, Denmark.

The Valley of the Giants Treetop Walk, in Walpole–Nornalup National Park, is 600 metres long and gives views of the canopy of a Tingle forest.

The peaceful estuary of the Denmark River is typical of many waterways in the South-West.

Karri trees can tower to 60 metres.

The Citizens' Advice Bureau and Tourist Centre, Albany.

Albany's Old Post Office, built in 1870,
houses a restaurant and museum.

A symbol of maritime origins in front of the Albany Town Hall.

Great Southern

wilderness on the whaling coast

The Great Southern is an area of superb natural beauty. In Albany, Western Australia's oldest town, memories of the wild days of whaling remain. Today, most visitors enjoy the magnificent coastal scenery created by granite headlands, coves of silver sand and the untamed Southern Ocean.

Natural Bridge is a feature of Torndirrup National Park.

A whale-catcher, memorial to the 850 whales killed during each year of whaling.

The Stirling Range consists of a chain of peaks, 65 kilometres long and 10 kilometres across. This national park is one of the best places to see Western Australia's fabulous wildflowers, for there are over 1500 species found on mountains, in valleys and across surrounding heathland. More species of flora are found here than in the whole of the British Isles. Around 60 of these species are found nowhere else in the world.

Above: A female Red-tailed Black-Cockatoo.

Scarlet Banksia, *Banksia coccinea*.

The Stirling Range is noted for the mountains' colour changes, influenced by time of day and weather.

From an early age, Steve Parish has been driven by his undying passion for Australia to photograph every aspect of it, from its wild animals and plants to its many wild places. Then he began to turn his camera on Australians and their ways of life. This body of work forms one of Australia's most diverse photographic libraries. Over the years, these images of Australia have been used in thousands of publications, from cards, calendars and stationery to books — pictorial, reference, guide and children's. Steve has combined his considerable talents as a photographer, writer, poet and public speaker with his acute sense of needs in the marketplace to create a publishing company that today is recognised worldwide.

Steve's primary goal is to turn the world on to nature, and, in pursuit of this lifelong objective, he has published a world-class range of children's books and learning aids. He sees our children as the decision makers of tomorrow and the guardians of our heritage.

Published by Steve Parish Publishing Pty Ltd
PO Box 1058, Archerfield, Queensland 4108 Australia

© copyright Steve Parish Publishing Pty Ltd

ISBN 978174021097 3

First published 2002. Reprinted 2004, 2005, 2006, 2007, 2008.

Photography & text: Steve Parish

Design: Gill Stack, SPP
Editorial: Ted Lewis; Karin Cox & Michele Perry, SPP
Production: Tiffany Johnson; Tina Brewster & Jacqueline Schneider, SPP

Cover: Perth city, seen over Southern Cross Fountain, John Oldham Park; Cape Leeuwin Lighthouse (inset). Title page: Boats moored at Matilda Bay on the Swan River. pp. 2–3: The lights of Perth city are best appreciated at night from Kings Park. pp. 4–5 Perth city skyline viewed from Kings Park. pp. 62–3: Stirling Range.

Prepress by Colour Chiefs Digital Imaging, Brisbane, Australia
Printed in China by 1010 Printing International Ltd

Produced in Australia at the Steve Parish Publishing Studios

Steve Parish
PUBLISHING

www.steveparish.com.au
www.photographaustralia.com.au